LEGO BIONICLE®

GATHERING OF THE TOA

Story by Ryder Windham
Art by Caravan Studio

L B
Little   aders

This
La

D0278233

LITTLE, BROWN BOOKS FOR YOUNG READERS

First published in the United States in 2015 by Little, Brown and Company
First published in Great Britain in 2015 by Hodder and Stoughton

1 3 5 7 9 10 8 6 4 2

LEGO, the LEGO logo, and BIONICLE are trademarks of the LEGO Group.

Produced by Hodder and Stoughton under license
from the LEGO Group. © 2015 The LEGO Group

Line art by Faisal P
Colors by Felix H, Kate, Angie, Indra, Ifan, Hazmi, and Rendra

The moral rights of the author and the illustrator have been asserted.

*All characters and events in this publication, other than those clearly
in the public domain, are fictitious and any resemblance to
real persons, living or dead, is purely coincidental.*

All rights reserved.
No part of this publication may be reproduced, stored in
a retrieval system, or transmitted, in any form or by any means, without
the prior permission in writing of the publisher, nor be otherwise circulated
in any form of binding or cover other than that in which it is published
and without a similar condition including this condition
being imposed on the subsequent purchaser.

A CIP catalogue record for this book
is available from the British Library.

ISBN 978-1-51020-053-1

Printed and bound in the United States of America

Little, Brown Books for Young Readers
An imprint of
Hachette Children's Group
Part of Hodder and Stoughton
Carmelite House
50 Victoria Embankment
London EC4Y 0DZ

Hachette UK Company
www.hachette.co.uk

.hachettechildrens.co.uk

Lancashire Library Services	
30118132633748	
PETERS	JF
£5.99	04-Mar-2016
ENE	

THE PROPHECY

It was pieced together by fragments, whispered to the people of Okoto thousands of years ago when they found the lifeless body of Ekimu the Mask Maker. The prophecy has been told around the campfires as part of the legacy of the Protectors, and handed down through the generations from father to son...

When times are dark
and all hope seems lost,

The Protectors
must unite,

One from each tribe,

Evoke the power of
past and future

And look to the skies
for an answer.

When the stars align,

Six comets will bring
timeless heroes

To claim the
masks of power

And find the Mask Maker.

United, the elements hold
the power to defeat evil.

United but not one.

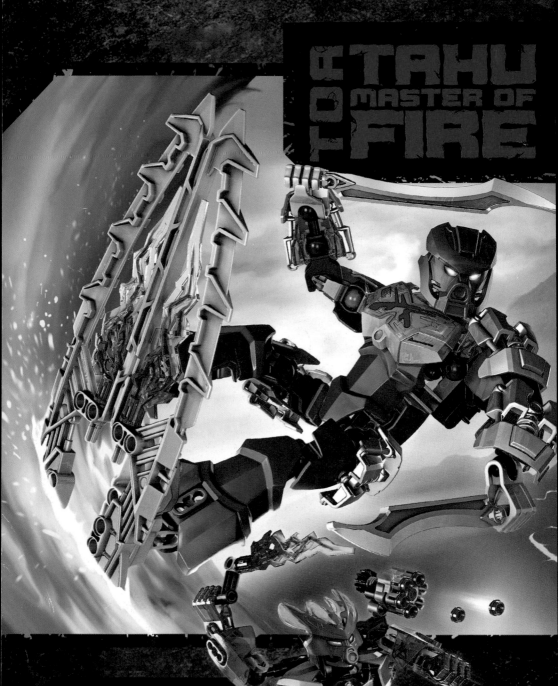

TAHU
MASTER OF FIRE

NARMOTO
PROTECTOR OF THE FIRE

KOPAKA
MASTER OF
ICE

IZOTOR
PROTECTOR
OF THE ICE

ONUA
MASTER OF EARTH

KORGOT
PROTECTOR OF THE EARTH

TOA LEWA
MASTER OF JUNGLE

VIZUNA
PROTECTOR OF THE JUNGLE

POHATU
MASTER OF
STONE

NILKUU
PROTECTOR
OF THE STONE

TOA GALI
MASTER OF WATER

KIVODA
PROTECTOR OF THE WATER

GATHERING OF THE TOA

"THE TOA INCLUDE POHATU, MASTER OF STONE..."

"...KOPAKA, MASTER OF ICE..."

"...GALI, MASTER OF WATER..."

"...LEWA, MASTER OF JUNGLE..."

"...AND TAHU, MASTER OF FIRE.

IT WAS FORETOLD THAT ALL SIX TOA WOULD ARRIVE..."

...AND EACH WOULD GO ON A QUEST FOR GOLDEN MASKS TO UNLOCK THEIR GREAT POWERS!

IT IS YOUR *DESTINY!*

OH. HAVING A DESTINY SOUNDS VERY IMPORTANT!

WHEN EXACTLY SHOULD I BEGIN MY QUEST?

RIGHT NOW!

ARE THOSE THE RUINS OF A CITY, IZOTOR?

IT **WAS** A CITY, KOPAKA, A LONG TIME AGO. BUT LIKE ALL THE GREAT CITIES OF OKOTO...

...IT IS **LONG ABANDONED**, AND NOW BUT AN **ANCIENT TOMB**.

DID WARRING ARMIES DESTROY THE CITIES?

NO, NOT ARMIES, BUT BY A CLASH BETWEEN **TWO BROTHERS**...

...THE **MASK MAKERS**, WHO DREW FROM OUR ISLAND'S **ELEMENTAL FORCES** TO CREATE THE **MASKS OF POWER**.

"EACH BROTHER POSSESSED A SPECIAL MASK. EKIMU WORE THE **MASK OF CREATION**..."

"...AND MAKUTA WORE THE **MASK OF CONTROL**."

"TOGETHER, THEY PROVIDED MASKS FOR ALL THE ISLANDERS, BUT EKIMU'S WERE THE MOST TREASURED."

13

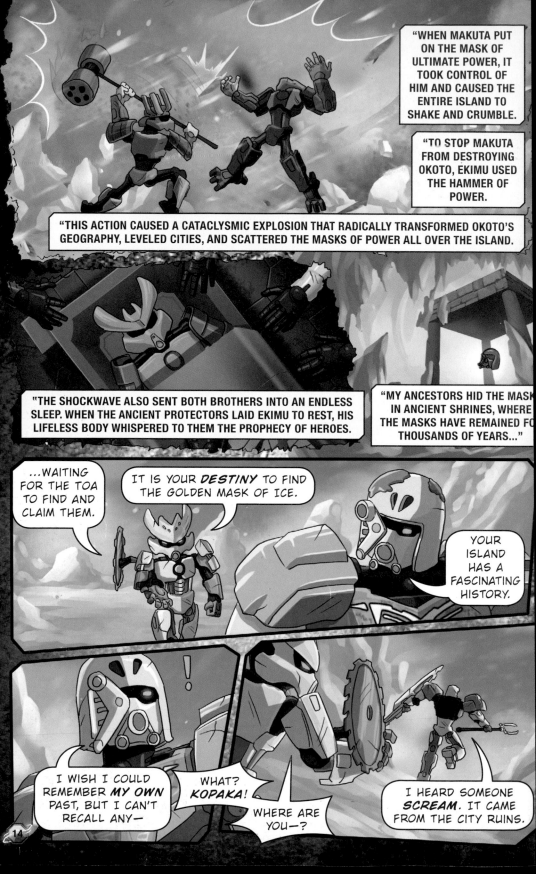

19

EVER SINCE I ARRIVED ON OKOTO, IT'S BEEN ONE BATTLE WITH SKULL SPIDERS AFTER ANOTHER!

I HOPE THE *LORD OF SKULL SPIDERS* GETS THIS *MESSAGE...*

BRAPPA BRAPPA

SKREEE

THERE'S A *NEW HERO* ON THE ISLAND, AND HE *LIVES* TO DEFEAT EVIL!

ACTUALLY, TAHU, I'LL REMIND YOU THAT THE COMETS BROUGHT *SIX* HEROES TO OKOTO.

SKREEE

YES, NARMOTO, I REMEMBER WHAT YOU TOLD ME ABOUT THE OTHER TOA.

THEY MUST BE EAGER TO MEET ME SO I CAN LEAD THEM.

OH? THE PROPHECY SPEAKS NOT OF LEADERSHIP, BUT OF *UNITY.*

BECAUSE YOU'VE NO MEMORIES OF THE OTHER HEROES, PERHAPS YOU MUST RELEARN THE VALUE OF *TEAMWORK.*

I'M CERTAIN THEY'LL MAKE A FINE TEAM SO LONG AS THEY FOLLOW *MY* COMMANDS.

—SIGH—

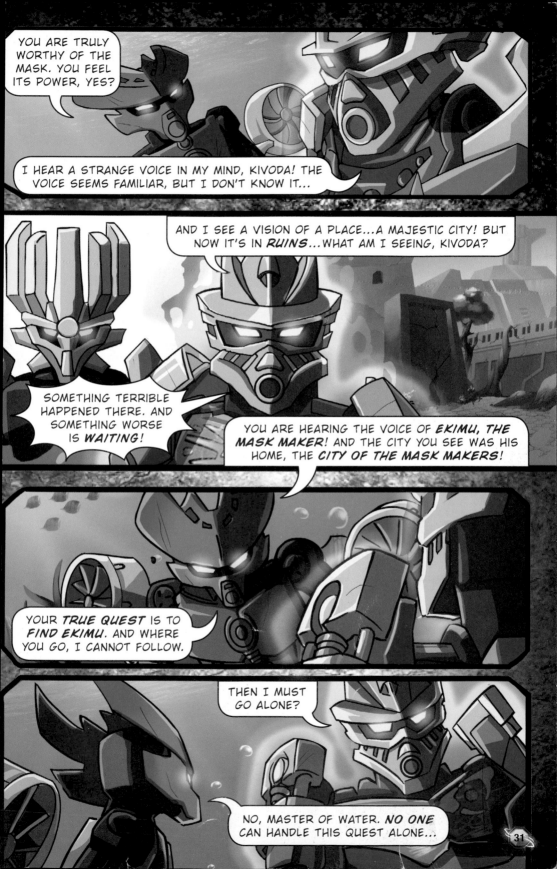

THE PROPHECY TELLS OF SIX ELEMENTS MASTERED BY SIX HEROES.

YOUR DESTINY, GALI, IS TO UNITE WITH THEM. TOGETHER, YOU WILL DEFEAT EVIL.

THE CITY OF THE MASK MAKERS LIES SOUTHWEST OF HERE, IN THE FOOTHILLS OF A MOUNTAIN IN THE JUNGLE REGION.

BUT KNOW THIS, GALI: THE CITY HOLDS ENEMIES WHO ARE STRONGER THAN YOU CAN IMAGINE.

YOUR MASK WILL GUIDE YOU THERE. GO QUICKLY, FOR EVIL GROWS STRONGER EVERY DAY!

POHATU IN *MOUNTAIN TERROR*

ALTHOUGH YOUR GOLDEN MASK GIVES YOU ELEMENTAL POWERS, POHATU, YOU MUST STILL BE *WATCHFUL*.

MANY *WILD BEASTS* LIVE IN THE MOUNTAINS BETWEEN HERE AND THE CITY OF THE MASK MAKERS, SO MAKE YOUR TREK CAREFULLY THROUGH THE WILD LANDSCAPE.

YOU ARE A BRAVE WARRIOR, NILKUU. IT WAS AN HONOR TO FIGHT BY YOUR SIDE.

THE HONOR WAS MINE, MASTER OF STONE!

WROWWL!

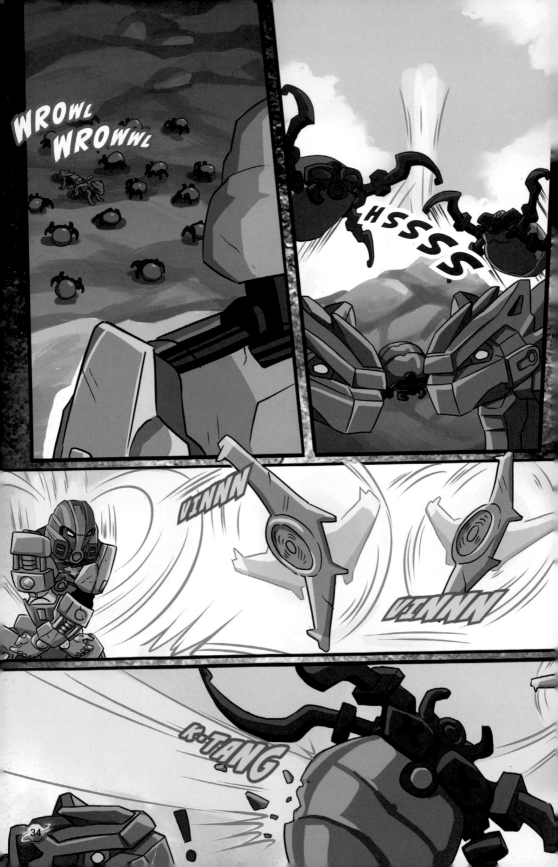

YOU REALLY DIDN'T HAVE TO WALK WITH ME THROUGH THE NIGHT. I'M NOT SCARED OF THE DARK OR ANYTHING.

LIKE I SAID, I DON'T WANT ANY PETS. SO YOU CAN GO NOW.

GO ON. GO DO WHATEVER "ANIMAL THINGS" ANIMALS DO. I'VE GOT SPIDERS TO SMASH AND STUFF.

YOU REALLY CAN'T TAKE A HINT, CAN YOU? GO ON. I HAVE A DUTY TO FULFILL HERE.

SIGH. FINE, I ADMIT IT. IT WAS NICE HANGING WITH YOU TOO.

I'M A STRANGER IN A STRANGE LAND, SO IT'S NICE TO KNOW I HAVE A FEW NEW FRIENDS. TAKE CARE OF EACH OTHER.

AND I'LL TAKE CARE OF THE BAD GUYS.

GREETINGS! I AM *TAHU, MASTER OF FIRE.*

THE *PROPHECY* HAS BROUGHT US TOGETHER UNDER MY COMMAND.

YOUR COMMAND? DID YOUR BRAIN CATCH FIRE?

I AM *KOPAKA*, AND I WORK UNDER *NO ONE'S* COMMAND!

I AM *ONUA, MASTER OF EARTH.*

I AM *GALI, MASTER OF WATER.*

I AM *POHATU, MASTER OF STONE.*

I AM *LEWA, MASTER OF JUNGLE.*

41

THE OKOTO

PROTECTORS GUIDE

THE PROTECTORS GUIDE

Many generations of Protectors have served as the peacekeepers and caretakers of the island of Okoto. Gathered around campfires, the Protectors recited the Prophecy of Heroes, which was first whispered to their ancestors by the sleeping body of Ekimu the Mask Maker after a devastating and historic battle with his evil brother, Makuta.

When times are dark and
all hope seems lost,
The Protectors must unite,
One from each tribe,
Evoke the power of past and future
And look to the skies for an answer.
When the stars align,
Six comets will bring timeless heroes
To claim the masks of power
And find the Mask Maker.
United, the elements hold
the power to defeat evil.
United but not one.

THE MASK MAKERS

Thousands of years ago, the brothers Ekimu and Makuta, known as the Mask Makers, used the elemental forces of the island of Okoto to create masks of power for the islanders. The islanders used their masks of power to shape their island, transforming it into a fantastic place full of wonders and beautiful landscapes.

The Mask Makers possessed special masks. Ekimu had the Mask of Creation, and Makuta had the Mask of Control. Although the brothers produced many masks, the islanders especially treasured the mask made by Ekimu. Makuta became envious of his brother's popularity, and came up with a treacherous plan to create the most powerful mask ever.

BATTLE FOR POWER

Although the Mask Makers knew that masks with more than one elemental power were extremely dangerous and difficult to control, Makuta channeled the island's six elements into a single mask, which he called the Mask of Ultimate Power. When Makuta put the mask on, its power overwhelmed him, and the island began to shake and crumble.

Realizing what Makuta had done, Ekimu managed to knock the mask off Makuta's face. The sudden disconnection caused a cataclysmic explosion that not only radically altered the island's geography—it also sent both brothers into a sleep that would last for millennia. The explosion also left many masks—including the brothers' masks and the Mask of Ultimate Power—scattered across the island.

MAP OF OKOTO

Once a paradise full of great forests and brimming with life, the island of Okoto was forever changed by the explosion of the Mask of Ultimate Power during the battle of the Mask Makers. The tremendous energy unleashed by the explosion destroyed the island's great cities and transformed Okoto into an island with six distinct regions, characterized by ice, water, jungle, fire, earth, and stone. Only the southern jungles, protected from the blast by the lee of the mountains, escaped the cataclysm.

THE GREAT CRATER

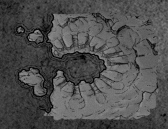

Once the site of a great capital built by Okoto's ancient civilization, and also the site of the battle of the Mask Makers, the Great Crater was formed by the explosion caused by the Mask of Ultimate Power.

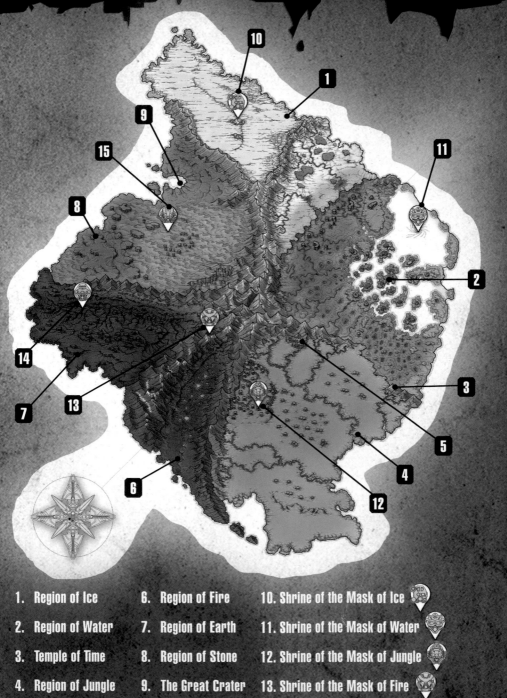

1. **Region of Ice**	6. **Region of Fire**	10. **Shrine of the Mask of Ice**
2. **Region of Water**	7. **Region of Earth**	11. **Shrine of the Mask of Water**
3. **Temple of Time**	8. **Region of Stone**	12. **Shrine of the Mask of Jungle**
4. **Region of Jungle**	9. **The Great Crater**	13. **Shrine of the Mask of Fire**
5. **Ruined City of the Mask Makers**		14. **Shrine of the Mask of Earth**
		15. **Shrine of the Mask of Stone**

THE TEMPLE OF TIME

Perched on the peak of a small mountain on the eastern side of Okoto, between the Region of Water and the Region of Jungle, the Temple of Time is the Protectors' most sacred place. The Protectors believe the Temple of Time is the oldest structure on the entire island, and it is among the few structures that escaped destruction during the battle of the Mask Makers. The Protectors also believe

that the temple mystically connects Okoto with other places, including distant worlds, across time and space. When the Protectors finally realize that their own powers are not sufficient to stop the rising evil on Okoto, they go to the Temple of Time to recite the Prophecy of Heroes and summon the Toa.

THE MASK OF TIME

Kept in a secret vault in the Temple of Time, the Mask of Time possesses powers that even the wisest elders don't completely understand. According to ancient legends, the Mask of Time is actually a fragment of a larger mask: It is the upper half that completes the true Mask of Time. The Protectors do not possess any records or illustrations regarding the lower half of the Mask of Time and are unaware of its location.

THE PROTECTORS

Six Protectors, one from each regional tribe on Okoto, are tasked with helping to guide the six Toa on their quests. The Protectors wear sacred Elemental Masks that have been passed down through many generations. Each carries uniquely personal weapons that were engineered for optimal use in their home regions. Because of their duties and the vastness of their island, the six Protectors rarely gather in the same location at the same time.

Protector of Ice

Name: Izotor

Weapons: Elemental ice blaster, ice saw

Protector of Water

Name: Kivoda

Weapons: Elemental torpedo blaster, two propulsion turbines

Protector of Jungle

Name: Vizuna

Weapons: Air elemental flame bow, sensor tail

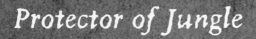

Protector of Fire

Name: Narmoto

Weapons: Elemental fire blaster, two flame swords

Protector of Earth

Name: Korgot

Weapons: Rapid shooter, two throwing knives, adamantine star drill

Protector of Stone

Name: Nilkuu

Weapon: Elemental sandstone blaster

THE HEROES

Delivered by comets to the island of Okoto, the six Toa are timeless heroes who respectively represent the island's six elemental forces: ice, water, jungle, fire, earth, and stone. Where they came from or who sent them remains a mystery, but their arrival was anticipated by the ancient Prophecy of Heroes, which foretold that they would come and save Okoto in a time of darkness.

Master of Ice

Name: Kopaka

Weapons: Ice spear, frost shield, avalanche skis

Master of Water

Name: Gali

Weapons: Harpoon, elemental trident, shark fins

Master of Jungle

Name: Lewa

Weapons: Two battle axes, two swords, X-glider

Master of Fire

Name: Tahu

Weapons: Fire blades, two golden swords

Master of Earth

Name: Onua

Weapons: Earthquake hammer, turbo shovelers

Master of Stone

Name: Pohatu

Weapons: Dagger, two stormerangs

LORD OF SKULL SPIDERS

An evil-eyed, six-legged creature, the monstrous Lord of Skull Spiders patrols and guards the bridge to the ancient City of the Mask Makers. As his name implies, the Lord of Skull Spiders controls all the Skull Spiders, using a telepathic link to make them locate and steal every mask they can find. The Lord of Skull Spiders spits sticky webbing at his enemies and is also the master of a powerful death-lock attack that can squeeze the air out of even the toughest hero.

SKULL SPIDERS

When four-legged Skull Spiders lock on to a victim's head, they possess the victim's mind, transforming the victim into a slave of the Lord of Skull Spiders. Although victims can be rescued if an ally knocks the spider off his or her head, and although the Protectors have mastered many fighting techniques to subdue the spiders, the spiders remain a terrible threat to the islanders on Okoto.

Blue Skull Spiders

Notoriously tough, blue Skull Spiders are not easily crushed by heavy weights or hard impacts.

Green Skull Spiders

Having developed X-ray vision, green Skull Spiders can find prey in total darkness.

Silver Skull Spiders

A subspecies of the Skull Spiders, silver Skull Spiders are the fastest.

THE GOLDEN MASKS OF POWER

Crafted by Ekimu the Mask Maker, the six Golden Masks of Power were among the many masks that became scattered all over the island during Ekimu's explosive battle with his evil brother, Makuta. The Protectors recovered the Golden Masks and hid them in six different secret shrines, and for many centuries they waited for the day when six timeless heroes would come to claim the masks. Once claimed, the Golden Masks give each Toa the unique power to control an element.

The Golden Mask of Ice

The Golden Mask of Water

The Golden Mask of Jungle

The Golden Mask of Fire

The Golden Mask of Earth

The Golden Mask of Stone

Solve This Code

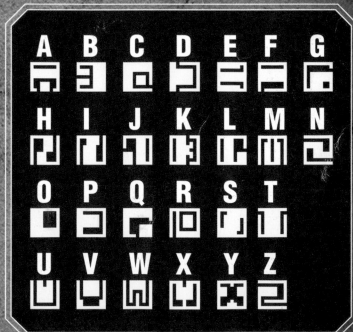